Heaven on Earth

By

George A. Hart

ISBN: 978-0-9840313-9-9

Heaven on Earth:

A Book of Morality

A Book about beginnings, endings, and eternal repetition of childish mistakes.

Introduction

Today the herald of man will come.
Tomorrow it will be the apocalypse for you.
Hail me, for I came, and I will come again.
Hail me, I am armed facing the sun.
Hail me, I have aimed the gun.
It's the beginning,
the end you will never live to know.

Part 1

[I know where the merry-goes-round]

You always flow with the breeze of life, though there are set-backs you still move forward. You may find yourself walking in circles, getting nowhere, only to look back in dismay upon your mistake. You should have learned the first time, never to let it happen again. Seal the crack before it gets bigger. Fill the hole before it gets deeper. Would you fill the crack with putty? No! Because it is too soft and the crack will pierce through growing larger. Fill the crack with cement. Would you fill the hole with soil? No! It will be washed away. Fill the hole with rocks. Also, just to be safe, mark the spot so you may always see it, so that you always remember it. Reveal these mistakes to your true friends, teaching them the way, so they can climb out of the hole with you. Always to remember your mistake. For if you forget you will not have learned the lesson, finding yourself walking in another circle, trying to climb out of that same hole. Remember, don't be blinded by ambition, you lead your way.

Now, I sit upon the floor. For I am as the dirt I walk upon. I know my mistake, so does everyone else. My humiliation is observed. Starting from a first level, I begin once again. Here as a fool I learn again, that my knowledge is truth. Your belief is weary of me. Do not punish those for that, what they can only conceive.

If you have lost your keys, the doors of opportunity have been locked. Thou has been shut out from life. If you're burning your bridges back, no ties shall you hold to help you. There you'll stand alone on an isle, cast away with the tide of denial. It seems the end, your only answer is to begin again. Making one more loop turning clockwise, moving forward. There you'll rise, higher into the sky. Once again, the sun is rising.

Every door I open, will be one, you can pass through. Every seal I've broken, will be one, that holds my key. When the treasure is found, let all the love go free. In time, they will all join us. For everyone must be ready to follow me, to declare you love all things, to mount the wind, for the ride within.

Every mountain I climb, will be one, and a foot hill to those that come. Every bridge I've crossed, will be one, and our ties ever closer. I am a man not unlike Jesus, yet as a Christ can I be real? For they've said he will come. I will be waiting!

I'm not here to hurt you, for there is no fear. I'm not here to kill you, for there is no way to die. I'm not here to screw you, for there's only love for me and you. What is this thing that, keeps us apart? What stands between us? I have only love, this isn't true, hatred is fear, through and through. This pain, will divide you. What stands between us? What is this thing that, keeps us apart?

There's no fear behind me, no fear in front of me. No-thing can stop me, no-thing can stand in my way. I can see everything, it was what I heard, what I knew to be. The thought of being free, I opened the door, I held the key.

I am your eyes, where you cannot see. I am your ears, where you cannot hear. You are the same for me. My eyes where I cannot see. My ears where I cannot hear. We are one. I open the door and give you the key. Don't ever lose it, don't ever forget. You have the power to set yourself free.

Upon this day I give you judgement. Behold the grand inquisitor. A mirror image, separation of the mind. For what you are is truth known by you.

If you have found pain, misery, and suffering, then you have truly found hell. You are there to learn something, which I will not tell you. For I can't, you must learn alone. Then we shall be together forever, finding peace, love, and happiness. Then you will truly have found heaven.

You have got your back to the mirror. Face the mirror, face to face. Are you not the same yet different? Every-body has two heads yet one. Search your shadow, find the truth.

Face me and face your fear. Don't turn your back on me, don't fear, fear. You are a shadow stemming from the light. You shall fall to your side, crawling out of sight. Just as I've pulled you, like the thorn sticking in my side. Blowing you away with the wind. Little seedling, you'll be replanted, where the soil has been turned.

All I wanted was, for you to love me. For I am the mountain, you will climb. I am the god, you shall meet. I am everything, that doesn't reveal itself to you. I am the shadow, I'm invisible.

You will, cower before me. For, I am the tower, enshading you. Here you'll learn, inner strength. For your fear has guided you. Again you'll be ready, for the light will be upon you. Here you'll learn, outer strength. For my light is ever brighter. When your fear comes again, you'll turn your back and the shadow will protrude. You'll see what you are and run for the dark, to join your part. So I say to you, besiege the day!

A wise man came to me and said, my son what are you building? And I said, an empire! And he said, be gracious in your tidings. For when it falls, it shall fall upon you.

[The Beginner]

You have to go out there. Like the bird who must fly, through the air. Pushed from the nest, belief must exist. Fear will let you fall, crack your skull on the ground. Faith will bring you back. Once again, you'll stand tall. The wind blows, the bird soars. Flying higher and higher, above the clouds. First comes the body. Then comes the mind. An illusion, for the beginner. All you must do, is remove the shroud.

My love is truth and my truth is love. I cannot lie, I shall never die, only to move on, teaching you to fly. Step back a little further, so you may fly a little higher. Every set back will be just one more step to take, when you move ahead. Spread your wings a little wider. Now, you may fly straight like a glider. Everything you learn shall be, every improvement you make.

And when the storm came ashore, it brought with it the seagulls. Hovering about and scattered, they were lost without their home. The older and wiser seagull realized, he must show them the way, for he knew. Shuffling them about, organizing them, he spoke unto the young birds. Remember, remember this today. For tomorrow you shall guide others. The ones pulled by the prevailing winds, left astray. Guide them back to the sea. Bring them home again. This is how it's been since the beginning. And this is how it will be.

Today it's cloudy. And the rain falls hard. The thunder strikes out from the earth. There will be hell to pay. Yet does not always the sun come forth. There are brighter days ahead. It is known the worst is still yet to come. A greater test for a greater achievement. A greater achievement for a greater reward.

Success can only come from progress. While the reality of life shall be a reality without a dream fulfilled. And without a dream to fulfill reality. To wish and never succeed. How far are you willing to go? What are you willing to do to achieve your goals?

You will pay the sacrifice due. The value of your efforts will prove you true. You will learn the rules. The game is simple. Break the rules, and be rewarded. A penalty for the price you will pay. Obey the rules, and be rewarded. Safe passage, for your worth will be known. Your achievements shall be greater.

We stand in line, awaiting our turns. The drawbridge will lower, then we shall step through. Only one more step. Anoction, into the absolute. The sleepless land of god. In boundless limits, set outside the incarnate. Endless rest yet there is no rest. He is god whom masters the game. Each time you play, your strategy shall improve. It's been said, dream until your dream comes true. And I say it's true, your worth has guided you. And I will have brought you through, Anoction.

[Those Who Are Willing Will Be Those That Learn]

When I come to you, I shall speak in the tongue of men. This tongue may be gentle or hollow. This tongue may be loud and vile. But I will be heard. Through men's eyes I will be seen, as they themselves are seen. I will teach those that will learn. When your will becomes weak, your faith in me may be lost. Then I could no longer teach you, the unwilling. My personal work with you, shall be done. I will be with you always, for what you'll learn, is what I came to teach.

And he'll drip. And he'll drip. And he'll drip. And drink from the river, the wine. And he'll drip. And He'll drip. And he'll drip. And drink from the river, the wine. He will suffer, and suffer, and suffer. He shall endure and live on.

Take the apple, for it rots in time. Watch and wonder how to stop the rotting. It is effortless, for you cannot stop what is of its own nature. Yet you can stop it from repeating. It has not learned to keep. Only to survive, through its seedlings. Why then keep it from repeating? Think of helping it to learn to keep. Plant them where the soil is replenished. The fruit was only to house the seeds. They shall grow new trees which, shall bare new fruit.

[Out With The Old, In With The New]

When I peeled the banana, I found it to be rotten. So, I peeled another. I still found it to be rotten. Then I peeled one more. This one was mostly fresh. For I still found a few bad spots. I took a knife and cut them out. Only to consume the ripened fruit. Its taste was delicious and my belly filled.

People are like good and bad nourishment. If you find one to be too rotten, move on to another, so that they may be saved. So that your taste is good and your heart filled.

I tell you a sad thing. We would all be best friends, if not for a paper like tool used in trade. While not to think of the consequences, this is a reality. For it shall come to show its true face, following the day after. For the love of money.

I ask of you, your need. What is your need? "Master, I wish to be a rich man." Are you, to be a rich man? The only rich man is a wise man. For your desire of greed has guided you. Today you are a wiser man. Though your will needs to be set free. What you ask of me is what a dog would ask of me. Take this dog away from me, now! For it carries disease. "Master please, please Master, I beg of you!!!" Wait, bring him back. The man who begs is willing and ready. Alright, I will tell you this. The richest man alive, is one whom is filled with knowledge. Learn my knowledge, for you will be richer than all your enemies. Take this penny I give to you. Make of it two, then four, then eight. Come back and teach me, what you have learned. This is a beginning. All must start somewhere. I have turned you, and guided you. Now, you're on your own.

When you're a child, this you cannot know. For you are blinded by your ambition, just learning to see, to read the surface. While far below a master's eyes can see. A fortune is not silver or gold, but a system to count your blessings. For if you have as many blessings as you can count, you truly are a wise-man, fulfilling your dreams. The wise-woman also knows whose truth is sown. From healthy seeds you have grown.

The sick shall always be sickly, until the day you're ready to be healthy. To take the step forward and reach. For help you will find, if you have asked.

The healthy shall always be healthy, until you have given in to be sickly. Tears of joy have become tears of sorrow. Your health is worth another tomorrow.

Don't ever lead blind eyes, by way of the question. For wherever there is, there is the question. What is life? Life is. What is the question? The question is. What is there wherever? There wherever is. Wherever there is, there is a blindfold to cover every pair of eyes. Is, is there, there wherever is, a pair of eyes to forever blindly lead. Is what question is, is what life is?

We're all here, no one knows the answer, no one can tell me why. We're reaching for the machine, yet we fight its pull. Forward we go, where the answer lies ahead. Many fears erupt when the personality begins to be lost. For fear of the loss of self shall always come. To join the machine we'll lose lower consciousness. To know everything is to be god and god does not show personality. God is everything, and to know everything is to be everything. We're like a springboard fighting our contraction. We expand in the opposite, only to spring back at the edge of maximum expansion. This is the natural pull, yet we are to flow with the breeze of life, we do go against, until recoilization. Basically, we go through life until we are snapped back into the nothing. The fear of death is the fear of loss of self. Linked to all humanity by mind transference. I bid you my knowledge. Do not fear the loss of self. For self is everything and every-one-self. We will join the machine, yet as children we will be children until the machine is upon you.

Part 2

[I Can See The Hide-An-Seekers Play]

When we were children we played games. We are still children, playing the same games, it just got a little harder. Everyone wears a mask, a disguise. We've built houses to protect us from our neighbors and the environment out of fear. This logic is an advancement yet a setback in our total freedom. In this shelter you create your mask, piece by piece. Building your strategy for this life, the live's quest. There you hide trying not to be seen through your mask, your disguise. Stepping out into the world seeking and finding, then being found, only to go back and prepare again, building a better strategy to win. When you lose others will know, becoming a fool in their eyes, for you have yet to learn.

Science is the search for god.
An god is the presence of life.
Death is the structure.
An its' foundation is ode.

You are beautiful, a living essence. Yet you are blinded by corruption, never to truly see. Life is a balance, tilt the scales and pay. Balance them and you will have recognized the beauty in life. This will outweigh your losses. You shall be free of your suffering. Then it was knowledge, your knowledge which will have given you the understanding, the sight, to see through the Dragon's eyes, which are your own. For you will have learned the understanding of balance. All force of life must be balanced or the scales shall tip upon you. Then you will bare the burden of a thousand sufferings, a wild wrath of terror and pain, a life of misery and destruction as you're rendered insane. Once balanced you shall truly see, to perceive as should. The Dragon will calm his breath to you. Turning his head away saying, "Remember, I blessed you, you hold the sacred soul. Let the blood run true. You've tasted my breath, now I be done with you."

Where has it brought me, swallowed by the Dragon? I thrive from within his belly. The beast is great, he shall shuffle and turn us, he shall twist and burn us, digesting us in his juices. Stemmed from life we'll learn, the battle you must win to earn and to earn you must win. Endless pain for the sufferer to begin. The last step is the great-test step. This will be the first step. A most valiant place to start is the end. For when the game is over, let us play again. Shall I not be a better opponent, less I learned not? My strategy will have increased. The odds will be in my favor. Now I will have won. I've become the best, I have passed the great-test. Plucked out as I'm spit from the belly. All my pain as I learn it was a game, the live's quest. Made to suffer, to learn, to begin. They were laughing and cheering, I had made it. I'm within the Dragon and he is within me. Part of the Dragon I am a god, a child with powers to master, to learn properly before being set free, setting myself free.

I see you up on your platform, fighting to hold your position. A power struggle, the better man or woman always wins. But you are nothing, a flea on the back of creation. I may be invisible to you, yet I am a god in the eyes of salvation.

I want to send you a message. I'm love, becoming possessive. I'm hate, becoming oppressive. We've a battle in all our minds, which may end in self-destruction. Helpless opportunity to create your own destiny. Let's journey together with the forces. Follow me into tomorrow's day. Let's walk into the sun. I'm the christ child, I have come. I'm the anti, no one is separate. All shall know god is the founder and your satan is half my soul.

Christ would have called me brother and I would have said, we are. For no one can hide the truth, be it we are brothers tied by our journey along this great quest. He also would have said, love me. For are we not to be loved, but loved by you. For that love is the same, loved within that which is loved without. I turned from the mirror and said, you are the evil, you are the good, loved within, loved without. Therefore, I shall give to those without, within and those within, without.

To believe in god, you must believe in yourself. If not, you are searching and you have found nothing. Then you shall find within and god will become as a voice to guide you and make the last judgement. The final truth will come from your mind.

Come in, out of the dark, there's a place somewhere for you. You cannot hide from me, I'm a white light, a magick power to believe. Destiny is something to conceive. Your dream, that's a dream until you fulfill the need.
When the Dragon spits, he doesn't spit facing into the wind, he spits from within the wind, away from the wind, never to stand against the breeze of life.

I want to be free, to dance in the street, sing my songs, and play my pipe. What's that society? A veil to hide me, from nothing. I'm alive, wake up and see. You can't keep me prisoner, there's no more fear.

I am my own person. I will live as my own. No one should come to me that would not come to themselves first. For you will be taken in by the religious, you will be taken in by the militant, you will be taken in by the political, and you will be taken in by their campaigns. What will be expected of you is change. I pray that I do not fall victim. This I fear, for I believe I may already have. Remember these things, so that you may escape them. The only change I will expect, is your own, when you're ready. If it be to follow me, then so be it. If it be to be my enemy, then so be it. If it be to make war with me and against me, then so be it, done!

Laugh and sing
An play your games.
Do you know his name?

I know where the merry goes round.
I can see the hide and seekers play.
I can hear the children sing to the day.

Run and cheer, join the sway.
An let us play, follow the leader.

Look, look, look at your parents. Look at their lives. See what they offer, work is your life, suffer is your life. Is this what you want? Is this how you want to live? A life of hell, a life to sell. Your life is bought. Is it worth it? Remember it's your life.

Look, look, look at me, come see my dream. I'm the pied piper, come to guide you to the overpass. Come follow me, come and see. March away, sing to impunity, escape into harmony.

I am the pied piper, come to life, come to save you. If you'll come, I'll take ya away, far away from here. No more pain, no more guilt, only pleasures I've built. Corruption, I'll wilt away. Pack your things, we're going to play, play a game meant to be played. Played with smiles, born to love. Come now or stay and play their games. Join their war, fighting for land in-between foreign shores.

I am the pied piper, come to take you away. To live in a land beyond Hamelin, beyond corruption today.

Can you believe in the fortune of life, Shangri-La, the fountain of youth? So many tried to find, Shangri-La, the paradise, so close to heaven.

I'm the pied piper, come to take you away, come to guide you, and make the path open, so you can follow through. Shangri-La, open your gates, let us enter, I've brought the children.

Come join me, walk to the sea. You-don't-want, a holy war. I'm the son, come to light, your way. Listen-to the piper play.

This is the world of folly, who shall we follow today? Will we be blind, to walk into the fire, every step of the way? Will we be led by misfits, causing our own destruction? By letting them lead us, beyond, into the next day. Tomorrow is a place of wonder, no one can tell the damage, whence men carry their own plunder.

Gaze into your crystal, to see your own misfortune. Look past the fold, see the sets of your life, for you have already grown old. Because truth comes, like the stabbing of a knife.

It's either paradise or hell, and work is hell. Working to survive, work or die, suffer inside. Man shall advance then subside. His masteries are greater than he ever imagined. Magick make-believe or does it really exist. Integrated into our daily lives, new names for new eras. Magick has become science, medicine, chemistry, etc., all contributes of the human mind. The question why? The answer thought, conscious thought. The question how? The answer collective thought, togetherness.

Let's walk a little further, take a look around. Breathe the air from this wildland. I assure you, its oxygen, not some exotic fruit stand. I can show you the secret, the one that makes you think, if I was not human, would I even care?

My friends it's all here, why do we find our way back? Life I say why life? It's the answer, it's the question. Who shall you trust? Who shall you believe? Your problem is the question, it's the answer to your dream, it's life holding you, death is lying, my friends we are never dying. Cry for life, a cry for death, an answer to my prayers. I'm the sign come to tell you, where is life, the death you'll never have? The shadow of man, I'm the final command.

I'm christ brother, you'll learn this in time. Turn the mirror, see the son. No one will hear me crying, no one will see me come. I'll be left there holding the blood of man. Alone, I'll walk through the holy land. All will be dead, only I will be left there, blood on my hands. Then the day will come, you'll see the provision of life. Beloved land, uninhabitable by man. God took me through hell and said, "This is your land, now your home." When I looked into his face, it was my own, and fire flooded from my eyes. Mayhem was cast into the high and invisible poll. Who shall be lord, who shall know?

Come join me, follow me, walk with me. For I know the world from which I've come and I know the world I sleep into, awaiting my very fate, which you and I shall meet. I must search out my destiny. By finding it I find my fate, which was never lost, but misplaced. For I know my end and accept it. I'm not afraid, the fear is being alone on a quest into heaven, paradise. For it's death you fear not life, proven by the instinct to survive, it's coming, it's beautiful, it's a surprise. You'll know when it's time, to die. The answer lies within you. Search your shadow for the truth. The mirror of time, the mirror of space, the mirror can reflect your face.

They're taking away my world, piece by piece. If you take away my world, you take away my life. Thus the future as always was, the dominating force always prevails. When before man there was nothing but the past in thrust. Forward endless dream, rotating the tower inside. I'm now man in link to change. From there to woman, link to link. From there man, bond to bond, link to bond, bond to link. Spiritual attainment, nirvana exhibit. I'm a god, for now and forever, never to deny my divinity. All hail the god in you!

[Pair Your Friends Like Your Enemies]

The day will come and your brother, may plot against me. If he betrays me, he betrays you and your brothers. For this is warning, if he betrays you once will he not betray you again. For if he plots with you against me, you betray yourself. Just as I said he will betray you again, did he not betray me. Why then would he not betray you and the knife will be plunged in your back? He will still be with me, and you will surely die. Because you have become the betrayer, and he shall tell me everything. So speak of this to none, for I will know if you're the betrayer.

In ancient times, to say another god's name would be blasphemy.

Atom-bomb, a leopard's speed – as fast as. It's foundation as strong as a bears feet – mushroom cloud. Its sound was like that of a lion's roar – king of the jungle. He shot fire from his mouth when he roared. That gave him its mighty arm of authority. To be hit by such a force, un-imaginable. The dragon is represented by fire, its fuel to combust – his throne.

When another is like their god and just as great, what do you call them? The Beast, because they are dogs at your feet and will replace you, if you let them. So, never let them. I shall be called, The Beast.

Oratory:
Lion -   Babylonian Empire
Bear – Media-Persian Empire
Leopard – Greek Empire
Dragon – Roman Empire / Rome

In ancient times, to say another god's name would be blasphemy. When another god is like their god and just as great, what do you call them, the beast? When one wants to rule and for their god to rule the other becomes like a dog at your feet, ready to bring you down. It is only right to protect what you believe if you truly know what you believe. I will be called The Beast and no dog will bring me down.

[The Death Gem]

Imperfection is perfection. For every line there is another. For every space there is an opposite space. Like a river flowing, it only moves in one direction. Like a wave in motion, it keeps spreading out. There is only animate and inanimate. Where there is a star, there is light. Where there is light, there is dark. Where there is darkness, there is birth. Where there is birth, there is the dawn. Where there is a dawn, comes the sun. From the sun comes life, and alive I will know death. Inanimation will ignite an unlit sun and a door will open. While a secret is revealed, life shall pass through the universe of division, calculation, and determination.

When men come they set a goal for themselves. Then they spend their lives trying to achieve this goal. Many will come to fulfill their dreams, for they are like the frog that jumps long. Many will fall short of their dreams, to land before the line, like the frog that has jumped short. But! I tell you this, every frog that has jumped short, will have jumped long and will jump long again. Here you will always find where there's one there's another. Some are tall, some are taller. Some are strong, some are stronger. Some are smart, some are smarter. Some live, some live longer. Some frogs jump long, some frogs jump short.

Part 3

[I Can Hear The Children Sing, To The Day]

Carpe Diem, enjoy the day! For tomorrow never came. I am dead yet I live forever. I am a god and shall be a greater god. Enjoy the life as it comes yet do not take it for granted. You may be looked down upon as your face shines and the storyteller will say you hold the face of granite. I will see through you, by your mark as all things leave a trail to follow and clues along its side. Love life, or it will hate you. Everywhere you turn there will be another hole in your path.

I am dead yet I live forever. I was once woman and shall be again, just as I am man. Every time I fall, I will rise. Come once, and again and again from this place of rest. Father, have I need for a marker. Fashioned from your image, I am as a god, then am I not a god and to be a greater god. Looking in from the mirror, outside I see my image, what I need and what I shall have. Fulfilling your need with the trust. Ancient days, the knowledge, the trust. My path will be easy to follow. I'm to zigzag my way through. You will know me by my mark. That you already know, but yet to be seen, yet to be heard. The gate to our kingdom, it's just the beginning, climb.

You can't cry about your problem. You can't be angered by your problem. You can't ever hide from your problem. For you shall fail your quest.

Calmly talk to someone who you love and loves you, of the problem you may have. If you find one with a tear falling from their eye, you could sing them a song from your heart. Comfort their pain with love.

If anger makes its way easily into your thoughts and aggravation occurs, don't allow it to take you. Even though your pain may be endless, you must think to yourself and believe you can endure this pain, for I shall achieve the next level. This is the secret of mind over matter or will power, in one word, endurance.

There is no escape as you've heard, you can run but you cannot hide. Wherever you go your problem will go or follow and haunt your mind. Insanity shall be your fate. You will succumb to sorrow and hate, love will be lost and drugs will be your hideaway. You have life to admit to, that is all. For when you do, the truth will be seen. You have suffered long enough, come and sing, let the music bring peace.

[Loneliness is an empty heart, my love will fill it up again.]

Your heart is like a wheel-barrel. When it becomes weighted down with a heavy burden, it will tip, always falling to one side, emptying itself on the ground. For this will have been your pain, overcoming you. The other side will have been your lost love, finding you alone. I shall come and balance the wheel-barrel, taking away your pain. Then I will fill your heart with love.

You shall never be alone, I will always accept you and with me your need will be fulfilled. Our bond shall last, eternal. We will be together forever.

Love is what we hold on to. I tell you the truth, there will be those that fear me. They shall be consumed by hatred. I will become as a demon to them. There will be those that accept me, you shall be consumed by love. I will become as an angel to you. God will have come and the Dragon will have given you sight. For he and she breathe, from within you.

I call the father of the man caldron. My spell is not of cast, but of spine. This is the law I live by, the balance and the neutrino. I am the light, behind me is the darkness. My past is a fireball, you can see the trail I've left.

Open the door to the power sect. I am the child, you never met. Come to me, now. I will give you, something you'll never forget.

The ocean of light-is draining. By day, by night-I come, burning, smitten, and blight. The Dragon gives you a kiss, will you stand to fight, the mountain that's true, the tree that en-shades you, the god you never knew.

Everything I've done, I've done for you. To show to you my value, to prove my worth. After all that I've done, am I still unworthy? This must be truth, because still my word means nothing to you and my folly numberless. For where I've failed today, tomorrow I shall try again. Now, I will avoid my mistakes, for I will have learned. No longer a child as I've grown an as a god I will be enthroned. But this day is still to come, for I see its glory and I've seen your shame.

All that I have done that I have done, for you. All through the pain, your laughter, drives me insane. What am I to do, when my words, are denied? Like the river flowing, my blood is spilled, by you. The pages of my books torn, to feed, the fire pits.

Give me the sword, I need to cut the weeds. Mighty tongue of thy lord, split the shaft of the wilted seed. Burn the plague, end the disease. This is my eulogy.

[Esprit De Corps]

Let my love be with thee forever, sealed with an atomic kiss.
Our love bonds us eternally.
No being of any size or shape, shall disarray our cosmic continuance.
Until completion into the absolute.
The shading of one, nirvana is attained.
Let us irrigate the land of the sun, where the children shall learn to love.
Peace shall penetrate the soul, the heart, just as the mallet crushes the skull.
Unified and inseparable we'll walk with the gods.
Infinite quota, the fulfillment of the lives quest, together.
Linked by the greatest power, the bonding of souls.
Never forget through the life, an eternal bond.
The giving of flight, made in the caldron of life.
All I can accept from you is your love, nothing more, nothing less, love.

There is a sun glowing from within you. Your beauty ripens the fruit, which shall bare the new flower, from which you are, flower of the sun.

I want to shed my body, like the snake sheds his skin. I want to be free, like the eagle flies in the wind.

This is the palace I built. Within it is everything. For you can live in my palace. I give it to you, but not as your own. I give you everything, yet you own nothing, for it is not your own. Your own is yourself alone, this is what you own. If greed is in your heart, in your blood, you have nothing, for I give you nothing. For greed is bleeding you, why then must it bleed me.

Everyone who says, "This is mine, and mine only," has been infected with greed. They will swear upon oath and it will mean nothing, as they are nothing. He who wants, desires, he who wills, needs and shall be given. If thee asks of you and you do not giveth, you are pale with sickness and have begun to rot.

Lust a wonderful desire, a good desire. Though if, you are sick with greed, this desire takes your will to do what you want, taking what you want. Then you are very ill and have rotted to the core. Your heart has become black. For you can call no one brother, because none are your brother. You are a thief, just as greed has stolen you. You will steal objects of wealth, you will steal objects of pleasure, and finally, you will steal objects of life. For everything has become an object to you, just as you've become an object to yourself.

The desire is the will and they are younger and older, foolish and wise. For it is your lack of knowledge that allows disease to manifest from whence you've learned. This disease attacks your desire. For desire is innocent and childlike, never to know infection. Would I hand a child a loaded weapon? No, because the child would most likely hurt himself and those around him. Then why do the peoples of the world arm their neighbors? For the quick buck of greed. We should be teaching them that it is dangerous to them and us. If another tried to take possession of their land, we should counteract the greedy children. Our goal should be to keep life, not wilt death. The law will be that every child is given the title god before their name. For you are not to separate yourself from god as god you are, and in paradise we shall live.

Brother, nothing is mine that isn't yours. This may not be the sane to you. For then, how can you call me brother, when brother means to be part of? Everything you hold and cherish, this is part of you. If I am your brother, I am part of you. To say what's mine is mine, is to say what you are, is for yourself. Separating yourself from me, why then call me brother, if we're not a part of each other?
I can call you brother. None, can call upon me this name, that name that is sacred, until the day you hold this belief. I shall be true, and I shall be true to you. Brother, I love you, sister, I love you too.

Listen to me, now. Who of you has come to me and does not wish to hear me speak? Does anyone of you here not want to hear me, why then should you listen? If you do not want to hear me, why then should you listen to my words? I ask of you who is unwilling to learn, you who believes you could be doing another thing, which is greater for your own interests, to take yourself away from me and do what you must do. Though I tell you, the day will come that you will hear my words and understand. For it is your will that brings you here to me. So, I say, if anyone of you does not want to be here or hear me, leave now and go away from me. Stop listening to my thoughts, stop reading into me.

The lesson I have today is to teach how a responsible will can become an irresponsible desire. All will is good, for big brother and big sister know no wrong to do wrong. When little brother and little sister know wrong to do wrong, they have not learned and their age means nothing. A child shall always be a child until, they know right, to not do wrong. Big brother and big sister know that desire is good, until they become infected with a disease called corruption. Since the human desire is innocent in the beginning, it is vulnerable to attack. If the human will intercedes corruption, the desire will build immunity. If not, corruption will take a foot hold. Sprouting first with greed, then to acclaim possession, and finally hatred. Greed will make your blood thicken with anxiety and longing to have everything your brother or sister has. When it has become in your reach, you will claim it as your own, even people. No person or being can own any other living being. Finally, you will want more to the point of envying your brothers and sisters. Hatred has taken you, where there was no heart, only emptiness from which pain has sprouted with the face of hate.

For anyone to become big brother or big sister, they'll have to learn how their desire can become an infected disease. Infection comes very easily to many and many may never understand. The will and the desire are the same. The will is the master over the desire, until infection has brought desire false control. The desire longs for control and when it seems to come, the infection is really in control. The desire only becomes the controller by becoming the will. By becoming the will, you become big brother and big sister, to always know what desire is good or not. The desire to have pleasure, such as sex, is a good desire, as long as it does not include a person that does not wish to participate. A good desire such as sex can become a trap for punishment.

When little brother was sent to the market by his family, he was given money to buy food so he can eat. He met a beautiful woman. She told him if he paid her the money his family gave him, he could sleep with her, have sex with her. The woman also had a family to feed, so she was determined. Little brother said. I can't, I have to buy food, so my family can eat. Then the woman flashed him her beautiful body and whispered in his ear, I will make it extra special for you. Little brother was drooling and could not resist any longer. He gave her the money and she slept with him, had sex with him, a fair deal, everything for something in this world. A few hours had past, little brother was afraid to go home, for fear of his family. Finally, little brother went home. His family asked him, where is the food they sent him to buy. He lied, saying some men robbed me and I couldn't see their faces, because they were wearing masks. Big brother came out and said, little brother, why do you lie to us your family, I saw you buying that woman's pleasure?

Little brother said, "No! No!" The family said, she beguiled him, then they started cursing the woman. Then big brother said, she has done nothing wrong, little brother has given in his will to his desire. For I have tested you and you shall still be called, little brother. You must learn that your family and yourself comes before your desires. I will go to the market and buy some food, so we may all eat. Little brother, you should be thankful. Tomorrow you will work hard for the food you have lost us. From now on your pleasures will come from your own pocket and your labor, you will not starve us again. For next time you will starve yourself and maybe then you will learn. Learn to spend wisely or be a fool, for what you've earned.

He who dares to mock me, then dare to mock the Lord. I am the judge of man. I am the judge of wo-man. King of man whom seats himself on my throne, with the crown of light. Fitted to the wanted need, a barren seed that wilts and bleeds. Like the desire that defeats the will, corruption breeds ill will. A corrupted seedling shall wither and die. A wanted desire awakens its friend corruption, to tempt you to what you want, not what you will need to survive. When the desire learns it cannot always have what it wants, it uses the will to call its friend corruption. While, instantly is filled with hate, plotting a destructive plan to take what it wills, as it took the will.

Hear me, for I tell you the truth, what is of this good and evil have you learned? There is no truth to this, for they are only names, they are brothers and sisters, they are mothers and fathers, and evil is their sons and daughters. Do you also know that, good can only breed good, and evil can only breed evil. Though good can become evil and evil can become good. This is because they can become one in your mind. We shall call good, our will, which is an adult. We shall call evil, our desire, which is a child, spreading silent disease. The disease cannot be eliminated by vaccine, only by recognizing its source and seeing the rotten fruit. Take the seeds and plant them again, this time in the richest soil. This fruit shall not be healthy, yet it will grow quicker. What it will learn is to keep, keep a strong will. This will is to survive and flourish.

Every woman wants to be queen. Every man wants to be king. Nation shall build nation atop itself. They will bury their dead and cry for god. The children are unwise to the disease that haunts them. For they will play a game, they will hope to finish. How can the game be won, when the game is alive and thinks for itself? When the whole is a whole it will divide itself again. A higher conscious derives itself from us. When a mass unit is separated, it thinks as many. When the unit is together it thinks as one. God does not separate itself from you, so do not separate yourself from god.

A man came into my home uninvited and said, "Who are you?" Then I said, would it not be more appropriate for you to introduce yourself to me, before questioning my authority?
"Why you should know who I am!"
If we were to meet in the street, I would pardon you with courtesy. To accept my courtesy, would be to accept me. I would know your heart is warm and I would know your true name. I shall call you brother.

Now I pardon you, for this inconvenience you have presented me. You may warm yourself at my fire, and you may join my family, when we seat ourselves at my table. For what is ours, is for all.

Some day you will seat yourself at my table. I shall call you brother, for that we'll be. Then you will eat and drink of me.

I've treated you as a king, then are you not a king? And must not a king need a kingdom, to rule over? Yet remember, your kingdom is mine, and yours the same.

When all is said and done, this you should have learned. Life's lesson is to deserve. From whence you are a servant, to thyself you bid your earnings. A rich man has knowledge, beyond all who trust his word.

[Open Your Mind]

Turn the handle on the door, and it shall open. You will find the answer, and love will be your cure.

You must live before you die. You must learn before you fly. You must be willing before you even try.

Forward you must go, facing the life happening to you. No place and no state can hide the truth. You're asking why and the answer is, why not? You were born, soon you shall die, the journey to the causeway through. Prepare to climb, prepare the mind. Ready yourself for the future. Complete your lives quest. Use the strategy you have devised. Prepare to enter the cosmic shrine. Death is coming, you're never to be blind. Face the end, you've prepared from now till then. You are split in battle, a pawn set upon a temporary board of life. Don't fear, for you'll forever be haunted by death in the mind. There always shall be one more day of sunshine, another flower shall bud and a man will come, a new day for a new life, meant to love.

The wind blew aimlessly across the land. Cold snows came down in what soon would turn. Their great forests all bare, behold the wasteland. I've an eye frozen in time, watching from a black sky, an ear to listen, the silent cries. Man lost in war, defeated by the veer. Ugly ghost staring blind into the mirror.

What was my goal? Only, to achieve. How will I achieve my goal, in this life?

1. I must learn to focus my attention. What will I focus my attention on? Remember, the only thing that matters is that I am here, now, in this life, to achieve, my, only, goal!
2. I must learn to follow through. What will I follow through on? What you are assured you can do, especially if you declare you can do it, or you will just be a talker, even worse, a liar!
3. I must learn to organize. How will I organize? I will file and clean. Also, I will schedule myself along with my duties, to which they correspond.
4. I will achieve my goal, very carefully and slowly, step by step. How will I carefully and slowly take step by step? By focusing my attention, following through, and organizing my duties and materials.

There are three types of philosophy. The first and foremost is that, that teaches. A well teaching philosophy reflects a teacher's image. Everyone is the teacher as everyone must learn. Second, is that which makes you truly think. For they resolve great thinkers that become great teachers. Third of all, is that which is the question. Some stages may fully consist of question, like people who go away from themselves and live outside. But, I tell you this, everyone who goes outside, will come back in.

Everyone who eats of the flesh of another living being has killed that being. For you are a taker of life. To consume the remains is to participate, take part in its slaying. The natural primeval tendencies to survive, are put to shame. While men and women strive for a better world and remember a great commandment, one not from above but from here, "Thou shall not kill." When it is just half-truth, it is half lied. The law should say, "Thou shall not kill any living being." For how old are we? Man the hypocrite, thou shall not kill, yet you'll kill to eat and survive. When this day comes and man has learned, it will be a new world, the true kingdom of heaven. While surrounded by death and killings you are blinded with fever. For you do not feed your heart, but you will feed your desire. Every time you eat of it, you will kill your brother and you kill yourself. The great dark apparition has won and you have lost your soul. Better for man to destroy himself than to destroy the world, though we do destroy the world as we destroy ourselves. How can man be so selfish? So I say, it all begins with you admitting to your-self you are a killer, a flesh eater, a primitive carnivore.

Are we the champions? Who will survive? Will man win the game? We can, if we try harder. It is all contained in the old saying, together we stand, divided we fall. This is not only the answer to everything, it is the ancient secret of completion. We will always be a step away, without this secret revealed, exposed. Also, to forever slip on that banana peel, dropped by your own hand. To shoot yourself in the foot after you've fallen, trying to remember why you bought the gun, in the first place! While thinking if you could get your hands on the person who dropped the peel, just like you load your own gun. There's no one around to blame, except yourself. For what is dealt by your hand, must be taken by your hand. You must take your own medicine, paying your own price. The same goes for, what comes around, goes around.

Individuality has faced face to face. Human differential has brought axe to sharpening stone. Fanatics will behead all that is different. This is the tenfold, gone a hundred fold, for this is history and history does repeat itself. Man can see and hear, yet how could he be so blind? I am the future, you are the past, a fool's anguish is a wise man's joy.

The great hydra has many, many heads. If you were to cut one off, would the great beast die? This is the law that states, it's not over until it's over, all over. The beast will simply grow another head to replace it. For it lives and nothing was lost. All of mankind is filled with individuality, yet he and she have forgotten that we are all linked in entity, being.

It's all the same, from a fist fight to a holy war. The entity is there and we are here, we copy everything the entity has to offer as perfection. The entity has one head and one body, we are its other. Every-body has two heads, one at the front and one at its back.

For one to truly be healthy, one must clean the body of poisons and toxins. Then you may begin to sort pains from anger, sores from decay, health from dysfunction. Once properly and efficiently purged of all alienations, disease will reveal itself from its murky bowels. Here with great will you can bring yourself to admit you are manifested with disease, so that you can move on to the next step. Physical disease shall be the hardest to overcome. Mental disease, disease of the mind can be cured by the will alone. For I not only speak of mental, but I speak of silent disease, that many have spoke of and I too have discovered, along with their cures. I have given name to them for what they truly are, to be taught to the world, just as others have done.

I hold a light. This light glows all around me. My light shines bright with knowledge. This knowledge is for everyone. Let me shed some light upon you.

When do you fulfill your need? Like you would like to eat, and when you want to eat. These things are the same, a wanted desire. This is the desire to consume. So, like when you need to eat, this is a will to eat. For this is the will of hunger. This is a fulfillment of a need of survival, the first and last instinct. Remember, will and desire are of the same branch, you cannot use one without the other.

[What Is Mine Is Yours, That Which Is Yours. Save that I am Just A Man. When I Cry, I Cry Like A Man. When I Have Died, I Have Died Like A Man.]

When the hour has come now, you'll recognize him by his words. I do not preach, I state a theory of completion. A teacher is a man or woman whom teaches. A writer is a man or woman whom writes. Then what is a man or woman whom saves? A savior is a man or woman whom saves lives, by which he or she uses superior knowledge. When the lord of hosts sends his greeting card to you, will you interpret his true message?

When you're afraid, you should know your fear. For fear is good and bad, it shall help you and hinder you. Fear will tap your desire to be, and to be undesirable. Desire is good at that, until corruption sets in. So remember desire will weaken your will.

While fear has presented to you an undesirability, never let your love be hindered, because of this. Let your love free to all, even the undesirable. For you shall face god, and you shall be judged. God is everything, thus judgment is. This you shall never forget.

It is not that, that you believe in which you follow, it is that, that you follow what you believe.

This is because, then you can be misdirected, by your own blindness, along the path you've taken. For to believe something and follow what you think, is different than to follow what you truly believe.

If you have become lost along your path, it is no longer your path, for it is many others.

Many times over your blindness may just be your ambition. For what you want is different from what you will need to survive.

Those who cherish material objects that are not necessities may be filled with disease, unless their path is clear and their needs secured. This lifestyle shall be a shadowy march, always abound to desires that surely test the will.

When the tide is strong, the opposition will be washed away, with the current. A muscle shall tighten, and a wall erected. Back to back, men and women will kill sister to deaden the pain. But your anger comes from within, and your undesirable, your repulsion strengthened.

If I asked for help and you do not give me the help I need, why is this? Am I not willing and ready to help myself, by asking for help? Is it not known that God helps those that help themselves? So then should not men and women help those that help themselves as God has shown to you, as Gods you are, and to be greater?

Men and women are of the same things and will have the same needs. For anyone to act against or for a single belief, race, color, creed, religion, and sexuality has brought judgment to themselves by judging others. For I have revealed judgment to you. To be for something is to be against something, for judgment shall creep up upon you. What you must remember is violence only feeds the fires of hatred. Hatred will beget many children toward its kindling. I tell you nature is a wonderful thing, but many of those who speak of and for nature and things that seem against its culmination, are blind to themselves. For if you look around you, we have separated ourselves from nature long ago, as Gods we lead ourselves. So then, if we lead ourselves into despair, we shall suffer despair. If we lead ourselves to annihilation, we shall suffer annihilation. If we lead ourselves to harmony, we shall suffer no more.

When true children have become adults, Gods together, never alone, you will see beyond the shell of men and women. What you will learn to see is the negative and positive reflection all beings admit. When many are grouped in a reflection, the circle of power should be felt. The more that are gathered among you, the greater the power reflected.

Monogamy is separation from the whole. While marriage is silent ownership of one another. One cannot own their brother or sister. I do not condone a monogamous lifestyle, yet I do not condemn it either. All must learn in their own time and place that vows are sacred and laws are holy. For this is the law, "do not separate unto me."
So then a marriage is the same as a holy war and I am only a voice that echoes through your mind. Without my word there will always be darkness. I still cross the valley and the light grows brighter. For you must face your greatest fear and the test shall be done. I the light of our lord god, you shall make a bond unto me alone. For you and I will be one alone with the lord, within.
"Just as suddenly as it begins, it ends."

My mind is my power, my strength of intelligence. My word is my sword, my weapon against. A gun shot is to be heard like the lion's roar. He stands high with pride and looks down upon me. For this is a sign that says I am ready to prove my worth. But I will come from below you and make you sweat. You will snap your jaw at me and break my bone and still, I will come! You will snap your finger and send your guard to me and break my bone and still, I will come! You will snap your bow and offer me a thrown beside and below yours. But I will not be put under foot by you. I will toss your crown and spit in your monkey eye. For I am a dog that cannot be touched by you, like a phantom I haunt you. For your reign is short, and I have made dust of you and erased your name from history. You crack a mighty roar as you lose control by way of your temper. I shall stand and roar over you and be heard over you and you'll fall and cower. The people will see this and bow down and say to me, lord! For I have come!

Time is only a memory. The past is from, the present is here, and the future is to. A memory is a map of what has been, before I was born, while I lived, after I died.
All that is stands at once. To know death is to know life. To know fire is to know water. To know hate is to know love. To know time is to know the future.
I do not stand against you, for you stand against yourself. There you will be consumed by yourself and fall. I will march with time and stand upon your ruins. Here I will build a kingdom and name it Heaven. They will come from the depths of hell and be risen, by my name.

If you have found the messiah in my words, in me, then you have found me in the messiah that lives and breathes. For I am just a teacher of wisdom and faith. Believe in yourself for the better and leave behind the worse. Stand with me and I will speak with you. Hail me and I will praise you. Defy me and I will blind you and persecute your soul. The darkness will spread from you and you will know me in a different light. Then I will guide you away from the others, so that you may learn alone and separate. I will honor you with gifts and the greatest is my love for you. So that now others will be jealous and envy you, they will hate you and be separated by their inexperience. For I have separated you by levels, like that of your age. The child shall hate and separate making ill use of their desire. The teenager shall begin to love and regroup, beginning to learn the will. The adult will see many things that need correction, by way of controlling the want.

When I see a man or woman, I do not see that his skin is black or her skin is white. When I see a man or woman, I do not see that he is a Jew or she is a Muslim. When I see a man or woman, I do not see that he is gay or she is a lesbian. When I see a man or woman, I can see them because I am not blind. I love without question, for I am you. When I find hatred because of these things, I know that I have found a child and shall look down upon you. So then when I find hatred for other reasons I will also know why, for a child cannot be determined by age alone. I can see the future, for I know time.

A store owner will put out a sign, to say that he is open for business. The people will see this and come in, to buy their goods with what they have earned, from the work they have done. So you will see, that much in the same way will the lord put out a sign, to say that he is open for business. So that people will see and come in, to buy his love and experience. Though it is said, you cannot buy love, but love can be earned, by the work you have done.

It's better to have a friend, and know your friend, then to have just another associate. There is one that shall call upon you, only when in need of something that you can offer. There is the one that shall be a monkey on your back until everything you may have that was worthwhile is exhausted. Then he or she will disappear like a magician, leaving you drained to move on and begin to leech another victim. These children are infected with disease. What does disease do? It spreads. So that now you are infected with disease, for that is what they are. They can only change by their own will. This may take a long period of time to fight off this disease. For it shall linger in your blood long after complete disassociation. For you may fall prey to their corruption and learn their ways. Through this you will practice their ways and spread the disease further.

The truth will make every man insane. Half-truths will blind you with shades of reality. Then lies will make men content, surrounded by fantasy.

There are those that wonder, and those that know. I have a name, it's inconceivable. My love has broken me, and my hate has famed.

Work for your brother and sister, so they may work for you. When you work for yourself, you are separating yourself out of selfishness. So must a priest pray for his brother and sister. For will you praise him as this is his or her job.

When men and women work together and for each other, they will become strong in mind. The strong mind will overcome greed and live for life, while many still live for greed. Together as men and women we should take our money, for this is our work and establish a trust. Your fortune is your shame. My tears will flow forever, until this day. Money is a tool of trade, not a weapon to degrade.

All the work you do, all the pain you'll go through, all the times you'll cry, this is what I mean by saying, "Let's end it all." Do not fret, for life will end itself. To walk a straight path will not be easy. What a march, for the strongest will, will succeed. This day is only to be declared a first, where life has only to be lived. In a world of sublime power, somehow and in some way, it's all a matter of sacrifice.

A wise man has many servants, who only service him. So when a man or woman has two masters, they serve neither, because they serve themselves. If one serves themselves they are wise. But if they are in your service and service themselves, again they have two masters and you are the false head. So then if your servant needs a house to live in, place a roof over his or her head. But retain the title, never to give away your power. So then if your servant needs a mode of transport, provide him or her with this need.

Also, retain the title, keeping strong your power over them. Then if your servant comes to you and asks for your title for his or her services, cut them loose from you. Your other servants will see this and tremble. For as much as it may cramp your heart to let them loose, cut their ties from you anyway. This is because you are truly doing them a favor, for they have grown wise by you. But warn them, just as a man may overdose on drugs, he may also overdose on knowledge.

Time paves a trail and in its wake, has come its dust!
Do you think its past over us? Where has it gone, to the future? Do you think we're in its hurl? Are we caught atop the fountain of time?
Dust dissipates and a trail cannot be traced.

This is goodbye, as all love will be lost. You didn't say it, so I will. No kiss, no hug, you knew I already knew. I think you let love blind you. Where was your respect for me, when you let him fool you? Well, I thank you, for I have learned something. Dress in white, if you want to fit in with the white. Dress in black, if you want to fit in with the black. Also, stay away from colors, for they'll confuse you both. I know you don't know what I'm talking about, but as I said, all have to learn the hard way. I will be here, but why should you try to find me? Do you really have what you want? Do you believe everything you hear? Don't you know, I will come, by waiting here? By this time, I won't be there, just in your mind. I'm not like others, I was willing to give up for you, sacrifice.

They always rise from below, to flip the coin, slipping through the cracks, climbing from beneath. A good foundation is sturdy, like a bears feet. Yet when the people start letting go, everything tends to shift. A hungry lion will then eat a lamb to be fit. He will stand tall to gaze upon his kingdom, preparing to sit. In his judgement, he will lash out a silent roar, like a leopard, closing in on his victim. To not see him coming, is a great surprise, for it will be too late. Then how can one stop what he cannot hear or see? For he cannot. When the coin has been flipped, fire will engulf everything, like the lion, the dragon, makes himself king.

He's the king of the mountain. He wields fire with this arm and hailstorms with the other. Millions die at his command. He is the king of all the land. His queen is a goddess. Her power to kill, is her stare, let any man just dare! Beheaded by your desires forsaken. For all the world is taken. I am the king of the hill. Everyone has played this game. Who is the master of their will? Don't lie, you're all taking the hill, be it as small as your will. Can you make it to the top? I will, run you down like a wildebeest, lay your bones at the foot, of my feet. They'll tremble and fall at my scream. You'll learn to respect the king and my queen, when the mountain begins to gleam.

Touch what you cannot touch. Taste what you cannot taste. Smell what you cannot smell. Will be, to know what you cannot know. I can touch reality upon which I can't.

Watch the green lights!

[Simplicity]

The possibilities are indistinguishable. It's so big, it's small and it's so small it's big. While the smaller it gets, is the smaller it will be. To then reverse itself, will be to, become large. While the larger it gets, is the larger it will be. Then large is small, small is smaller than large and small is large, large is larger than small. If you are large, you are small many more times. If you are small, you are large many less times. The greater the space, the less we occupy. The lesser the space, the more we occupy.

[Atoms and Elements]

We figured out how to break them, and we know what happens. We haven't figured out what they're made from, most obviously energies. We just call them what we name them, to give them order and classification. So from where do they come, the nill? I believe they come from one source element, through which they separate upon heat and friction energies. We haven't figured out how they're made, though we've learned to mix them or manipulate them to create new ones. This will soon enable us to synthesize elements, but we won't really unlock the cosmos until we can make them from scratch. When we fully understand how and what they're actually made from, we will know their original source, knowing how it all came to be.

Trust is their money, they can't live without. I am your other self, speaking to you. Buttons are gears, tightening the screw, in your head. If you want to rise higher, follow me general. Machines will break down, for none carry a lifetime warranty. But that's all you have and tomorrow it may be up. Put up your pen, and put up your voice. Come to me and deliver the order.

Life is nothing new, and death is nothing old. Your dreams are not yours, and your thoughts before. It's gonna happen, open the door, you'll see me. Your god has eyes of fire, that rain tears of desire. Because when all was dark, you were alone. There you survived by your will, alone. For then came a light and filled you. While you became consumed, your emptiness was soothed. A great longing had been put to rest and there you achieved a goal, love! Then love broke and moved on. Your emptiness returned and your desire born. For you could not be alone no more, so you chased the light on and on. Through your desire to have it, hate culminated inside. So then hate chased love, and love went on and on. Every once in a while the light will stop to rest and the darkness will catch up to it. Soon as the darkness thinks it's got it, the light slips away again. For it is impossible to catch the light, it just moves too fast, only another light can catch the light. A man killed someone and people asked, why? So god spoke up and said, "For something he cannot have! Stop chasing the light, it will come to you."

This is the truth, there is void and emptiness. Here it begins, at the mouth of every road. By the time you got there, there already was a beginning and an end. So forth you had gone, so seek its treasures. Remember, in man's words are magick meanings, set within during the beginning of knowledge. Treasures have been found and treasures have been lost, just as our knowledge has been found and lost. Love has been found on your path and it will be lost. Life will grant you and death will plant you, take away all you gained. Though through your work your children will be powerful, they may make the same mistakes. This is because children never listen to experience as they are too busy trying to experience. Do not wrong others or you will taste the wrath and feel its sting, while wisdom laughs, you'll see. Defend yourself with sword and shield, make your pen your sword and paper your shield. For books are your greatest weapons and death your greatest enemy. Here it ends at the mouth of every road. This is the truth, there is void and emptiness.

[By this oath I am bound]

I join this coven with my heart and mind. I join this coven with my body and soul. I join this coven with my knowledge and property. I join this coven with my life and death. Through my dedication, devotion, power, and conviction, I shall become one with this coven. I agree to obey its laws and to never separate from this coven stead. So like that of a marriage of men and women, I am so forth bonded eternally with breath of the Dragon's breath.

This here is the oath I have written. So here in the days of tomorrow, a ceremony will be held. For this is the inauguration of our newest members. This here is to be your greatest and proudest day yet. Let us celebrate as we bring our brothers and sisters together, uniting under the sun. Forever will be our names and these days we live, we'll be honored by all who climbed with us. From the dust I have become and to the dust I have begone. The day will be, that all shall burn their bridge with death and peace and harmony will succumb. Though fires will burn and everything trampled, many will survive.

I need eyes and I need ears. What do my eyes and ears wish to see or hear? So as I see and hear I shall also smell. I need a mouth and I need hands. What does my mouth taste to speak and my hands feel to wield?

Let the show and tell begin.

Men and women have been in-caged for so long, they don't really know what freedom is. For many become the tormentor they so despised, many create a tormentor, to close the walls around them. A jailer to lock your cell, into your own misery. Misery is only yours if you let it be yours. Once free from your own tormentor, you can open your eyes to see true freedom.

Buried by torment, say to this mountain, move! For it will get up and walk away. It was only there because you let it stay, like the fool who shares with ingrates.

When one builds themselves a prison, it's another form of escape. For it will only get darker and your pain will force you to face what you've been trying to escape. Time will stand still for you, while an eternity will pass. What you will learn is that, there is no escape, yet there is one way out.

He who has worked hard, will be strong. He who has thought long, will be smart. He who endures, will survive. He who wills, will be king.

For in the dawn shall come a new day and a new kingdom, for he who lives up to his full potential.

I am not a worm, that you may step on. I am a man, the god of men. I am a teacher, the god of men. I am a God, the god of men. I am that, what I am.

When I say men, you as women, should see women. For without you, there would be no men. So then here me, for here are your powers. Praise the God of wisdom, for he is within.

When the dead rise from the grave, they must feed from the living, just as the living feed from the living. So then what is to separate the dead from the living? How will men know, if the dead walk among you? The living shall be nourished by the living and the same in return. For what has been taken out will be put back in. The dead shall be nourished by the living and nothing shall be returned. Then like a thief in the night who has stolen your breath, you will be drained of life. For the dead shall multiply among the living, spreading their plague. Even the great stalkers shall become prey, as the mighty shark carries suckers, feeding upon the richness of your blood, your wealth.

Arrogance makes you ignorant to the things that truly are important, like friendship. So remember when one is arrogant and ignorant towards you, don't let it blind you in the same way, being arrogant and ignorant in return. Ask them what is the problem and show to them what is important and the ignorance of their actions or you to will be like them, blinded by false principles. So like the bird with a broken wind falls from the sky, you will tumble from your plateau. For there's nothing you can do, but see your own foolishness and feel the pain from your self-inflicted wounds.

You may fall a thousand times before you learn this lesson. For here it is written, now learn its value, so you do not repeat your mistakes.

My voice is thunder, for I cannot die. I am my words and my words are me. I will come to you, burning my name into your soul. So I always exist and have power beyond. When you look at yourself, you will see me and as others look upon you, they also will see me, because I am within you, as you have tasted my words and touched my soul.

I am the wizard who will appear in nightshade. For words are powerful and names more powerful. Call upon my name and I will rise to greet you. Listen, for my voice will be heard.

[When I asked the Christian Priest]

Father, tell me, what is worth more, a hand full of gold or a hand full of love? Then he said, "Love, my son."

Father I tell you, here neither is worth more, for one can't go far without the other, in this place of worship. For father, you truly are a rich man, one without expenses.

Father, do you have eyes like mine? Do you have ears like mine? Can you see what I see? Can you hear what I hear?

I can see that your riches are only temporary. This is because I can hear your superiors calling you with a quota to meet. So I say, here is your devotion, like you said, love is worth more, as that's all you'll get from me.

The world is full of greed and you ask where is all the love? For I tell you, they are keeping it to themselves. Whoever is full of greed, is full of love, for them self.

When I speak my philosophy, I speak the highest thoughts. For anyone who is a stepping stone, will tomorrow be part of the foundation. If you are part of the foundation, you will be buried, by advancement. Though you always have the power to break yourself free, by learning. Then you will feel a weight lifted from you. They who have built upon you will not fall, but will not let you from their sight. There will come others with the same ploy and you will recognize them immediately. Do not let them pass by way of you. For you are a giant and they know they must go around you.

My knowledge has tormented me, to the dismal reality. I am only tormented, if I let myself be tormented. I only know reality, if I let myself know reality. Every creature must follow laws, like that of men. Every creature has instincts, like loyalty, honor, bravery, dignity, and respect.

We are the only creatures that put our laws in stone. So begins the worship of an order.

The authority sets down the laws, for they are the power. So it is said, who made the rules we are to follow? This was a task for the highest order, as many proclaim God to be. What a reflection for men to see, this is my authority.

Life is a flight from death. So like a game to win, you stand to gain a secret key to the puzzles frame. I am immortal, but I find myself locked in a greater game.

Once you've solved the mystery, there shall come another. Then like a good detective loves to solve, you'll be driven by ambition to unveil a more complex mystery. For this is what you will be faced with, as you climb through the dimensions of oblivion.

It's so vast, everything becomes oblivious through time. Our will to survive is so strong, we have broken through the walls of nature. So from here on, we should call it, human nature. This term has been used throughout, the key to our escape. Remember, escape is only a temporary word, for you must realize you have only entered a larger cage. So as an old saying goes, hit your enemies in their sleep. For death will come to men and their cities when you lower your defenses, to the hand of relief. For pleasure is poison and pain your drink. Every city has children and all children will live to enjoy. I have counted my breath to the last. I have seen the vision clear, for extinction shall succumb. I have seen above and I have seen below. Come children, for you will climb with me. The road to God is the road to order. The road to nothing is the road to chaos. For God is order and I have spoken.

[My Song ?]

Do you know, how many loved me, loved me, loved me, in the past?
Do you care, where I've been?
Do you care, what I know?
Do you care, who I've been, what I've done?
Do you know, I'm the chosen one?
-

Whoever said, this is the pick of the litter, was born the runt.
Whoever said, this is the juiciest apple, is rotten to the core.
You're, a hypocrite, and I'm going to nail you to the floor.
Here is your puppet leader, dancing to the beat.
You, better be ready, I'm going to stomp you with my iron feet.
Here comes the militia, destined to defeat.
Jesus said to love, but it's hard to see the beauty with you, blocking my view.
Here comes the Master, spouting the truth.
-

Order is alliance, which is control.
Control creates defiance, which chaos must dethrone.
If I am the Devil, I was a God, worshipped in stone.
King after King you'll tumble and God after God you'll fall.
I am the knowledge, for I am wisdom, standing tall.